I Look To The Gentle Rain:
A Book of Poems and Writing Prompts for the Aching Heart

Written By Liz Newman

I Look To The Gentle Rain: A Book of Poems and Writing Prompts for the Aching Heart-1st Edition

ISBN: 9798853796515
Imprint: Independently published

Dedication

To every aching heart learning to honor the tension of great love and great loss: I hope you find words here that resonate with your heart, bring you comfort, and remind you that you're not alone.

To my family and friends who have been such unbelievable supporters of my writing: Thank you for your encouragement every step of the way. It has meant more than I can express.

To Dad: I will always carry your love and legacy within my heart. I miss you more than I have the words to say. I hope that the way I am choosing to honor and remember you is something you would be proud of. I love you immensely.

Preface

When we suffer a deep loss, we find ourselves face to face with an unpredictable and nonlinear sky of mourning.

Some days, all looks dark and the rains storm around us with little reprieve. Other days, things feel lighter and calm until an unexpected situation or memory reactivates our grief and the pain soaks our hearts in sorrow all over again.

Instead of tidy stages and predictable progressions, grief is immensely personal and unpredictable. And while it isn't something that ever fully goes away, we do start to see some of the ways it presents itself in our hearts and what helps our processing the most on the darker days.

Some sources of shelter and support are resources such as therapy, prayer, grief groups, trusted friends, and journaling. Each person will have a unique path and require different resources as they journey through this difficult terrain.

This book, as well as my first book "I Look to the Mourning Sky", are not meant to be "how-to grieve" books or prescriptive in any way. Rather, they are reflections about a journey: one that may be similar in some ways to the one you find yourself on as well.

I know our experiences with grief are deeply personal and unique to each of us. And we will have different ways of processing and different paces for the journey.

But my hope for this book is that it can be a gentle friend to you as you journey through your own uncertain terrain of loss and look up to your own sky of mourning.

My hope for this book is that bits and pieces of these poems resonate with your heart and make you feel seen and understood for a moment.

My hope for this book is that it can remind you that it is okay to grieve. It is okay to process in your own time and at your own pace. And it is more than okay to ask for help along the way. As a matter of fact, I think that is so incredibly brave.

Those who have known loss know that it extends far beyond the first year. It remains. It persists. It continues.

But the unexpected and beautiful truth is that the love also remains. It persists. It continues.

Some days, the heartbreak feels especially fresh and painful. Other days, it seems to settle into a tender ache.

But, while you look to your mourning sky, may you find that there are also days that feel like a gentle rain: soothing, healing, nurturing. Days that seem to grow the hope in your heart you never thought could make it through the darkest days. Days that honor the tension of grief, gratitude, love, loss, and every other heartbreaking and heartwarming moment along the way.

Days that remind you of the Light and the love and the hope that can still greet you on your hardest days.

This is unfamiliar and uncharted terrain: but may we journey gently with one another every step of the way.

-Liz

Table of Contents

Section Two: The Ebbs and Flows............................31

Section One:

The Tender Ache

Navigate

There's an ache
In my heart,
No amount of time
Could undo.

As I've had to learn
To let go of the pieces
Of myself
That I lost
When I lost you.

So much of
Who I was,
Was because of you
And now I must
Navigate that loss, too.

The Same

And through the tears that fall
Like a sorrowful rain,
I realize that I will
Never be the same.

The swirling storms of grief
A downpour of pain.
I realize that I will
Never be the same.

The dark skies of loss
Signal how much has changed.
I realize that I will
Never be the same.

<u>Forever</u>

Forever
is a long time.

It's a long time
to love someone.
It's a long time
to miss someone.

When we lose them,
It becomes a long time
to do both.

Your Love

Your love
Was safe and familiar
It made me feel
Seen and stronger.
When you left
My peace of mind
Went with you.
It's hard to navigate
All these spaces
Without you.

A Lifetime Longer

For we all are given time
In various amounts.
And we all do our best
To make each day count.
But what a tragedy it is
When that time runs out
Much too soon
And much too fast,
Oh, how I wish I could
have made it last
For a lifetime longer
Than you got to have.

Loud

And in the quiet,
I hear the echo
Of your absence,
In the stillness,
In the silence,
My heart aches with emptiness.
Loss is so loud.
Oh, loss is so loud

Observer

And when an observer
Looks from the outside in
They won't know where to begin,
Because they haven't been
Where you have been.

If Only They Knew

If only they knew,
Grief is not something to get through
but something that evolves
And changes alongside you.

If only they knew,
The road of loss is overwhelming and lonely,
An isolating and dark path
Full of painful uncertainty.

If only they knew,
How much "being there" can bring hope,
How much simple presence
And reaching out a hand
Can console in a way
Little else can.

If only they knew
There's so much more to loss
Than what the eye can see.
There's so much more to grieve
Than you ever realize there would be.

If only they knew.
If only they knew…

The Landscape

Grief tends to trickle
Into our routines,
Our hopes, and our dreams.
Loss shifts the landscape
And changes everything we see.

It's a lot for a heart
to wrestle with.
It's a lot for a heart
To grieve.
It's a lot for a heart
To navigate,
This soul-deep
All-encompassing ache.

Debris

On the days I felt my world shattering,
I thought the pain was
Crumbling at the feet
Of the people around me,
The pieces splintering inside of me.

I remember watching people
Tiptoe around the pieces
With side-long glances and distance,

All I needed was a pair of eyes
To meet mine.
For someone to be brave enough
To walk among the debris
to get to me.

The Grass Has Grown

I remember when
The dirt still grieved with us
Before the soil settled.

When the pain was as fresh as
The flowers that still lay
At your grave.

But now, the grass
Has grown.
That simple fact
Fills my heart with an ache
Like I've never known.

As though we watch time pass
Through the changes in the grass.

The grass at your grave
has grown.

Not Just a Date

It's not just a date on the calendar.
It's the one your heart breaks for
and every fiber of your being remembers.

It's not just a date on the calendar.
It's the one that changed everything
about each new year that you enter.

It's not just a date on the calendar.
or a painful alert on your phone.
It's so much more than the cold,
hard realities of a date on a stone,
but a soul ache felt deep to the bone.

If you find your heart heavy
as you reflect on that day,
If you find your soul weary
as you sit in that pain,
If you find your eyes teary
as there's so much to say
as you relive old memories,
and mourn the ones
you thought you'd make.

Your body, well-attuned
to the ache of this anniversary.
A day that became a wound,
The pain of such permanency.

May we proceed gently
with eyes full of empathy.
May we bear witness to these dates
And the complicated storms
of grief they create.

May my eyes meet yours
as you look at that day
with fear and fresh sadness
and emotions you can't quite name.
May my eyes meet yours
and may your heart hear them say:

"No, it's not just a date on the calendar."

Another Holiday

Another holiday without you
And it hurts just like the last.

It hurts to think of
a future without you
And it hurts to linger
too long in the past.

Time passes but
I'll never be past it.
Grief comes and goes
As it sees fit.
And I do my best
To face it.
I'll always do my best to face it.

I love you
I miss you
It hurts here without you.

But it helps
To remember,
To talk about you
To know there are others
Who hurt this way too.

To acknowledge
The ache
May always be there
But your love will be with me too.

<u>Tears</u>

Like the floodgates
Being released,
Sometimes I need to
Let the emotions
Pour out of me.

The tears flow.
The tears fall.
The tears feel
Like the only way
to express it all.

Your Birthday

It's your birthday,
But you're not here to
celebrate.

No more lights flickering
On buttercream
covered cakes.
No more
chorus of voices
Singing of what a
difference
Your presence makes.

No candlelight.
No warm smile.
No sweet celebration.
Sorrow has settled in,
Oh, sorrow
has settled in.

A day that
used to bring such joy
Is now so hard to face.
My heart, it longs to
honor you
But also, deeply aches.

But no matter
how I choose
Or do not choose
to celebrate
With tears or with song,
With silence
or with cake.

This day is still yours
And your love
is still mine
And that bond
will never break.

It's your birthday,
But you're not here to
celebrate.

But the cherished
memories flicker
And light
my darkest days.
Your voice
sings in my heart,
A reminder of what a
difference
Your love still makes.
And I'll carry it with me
Today and every day.

Broken Bone

It's like a broken bone
That never healed quite right.
An ache that I feel on cold days
When the chill of a memory
Dances up and down my spine.
Surprising me with the way
It can still induce pain
Even after all this time

Waiting Room

As I sit
In this familiar place,
The memories
snap into view.

As I count,
and recount the moments
Of being here with you.

My whole body remembers
The walls,
The sounds,
The panic,
Awaiting any news.

And that one
Impossibly
Small
Impossibly
Stifling
Waiting
Room.

How Long?

I wonder how long
It will take
For me to smell flowers
And not think
Of a funeral home.

I wonder how long
It will take
For me to
not feel like
My heart is going to hammer
Out of my chest
With every ring of my phone.

I wonder how long
It will take
For me to look at your room
And not feel a pit
In my stomach and
Feel so deeply alone.

I wonder…

How long?

After the Heartbreak

And after the heartbreak
Comes the ache:
The ache of a conversation
Gone unspoken with you.
The ache of a moment
When those we collected
Feel too few.

The ache of reality
And its reminders
That overwhelm my mind.
The ache of wanting
Oh, so desperately
To travel back in time.

The ache is persistent.
The ache is relentless.
The ache seems to
Always be with me.

But I know
That this kind of ache
Only finds its home
in the hearts
That have felt
Love deeply.

To Press Play

There are days when I can't
Find the strength to press play

When the joy of the music
Feels too far away.

When my heart skips a beat
Without rhyme or cause
But on those days
I've learned it's okay to press pause
To wait for the chorus to not feel so wrong.
For my heart to feel ready to sing along.

So, I can give myself permission
To pause and process,
To know that the music
Doesn't mean any less
And that the lyrics and notes
Will still explain and express

The things that we've felt
The beauty and heartbreak they bring
The songs that somehow understand everything.
The melodies will return to us
They'll echo and ring
And we'll know when we're ready
To join in and sing.

The Painful Question

"How do I do this without you?"

How does anyone continue
In a story that ended
Before it was supposed to?

The Layers of Loss

Loss of normalcy.
Loss of hopes and dreams.
Loss of the person you thought you'd get to be.
Loss of roles.
Loss of routines.
Loss of opportunity to make new memories.
Loss of comfort.
Loss of security.
Loss of so much more in between.
Loss goes so much deeper than what anyone sees.

It goes so much deeper
Than anyone sees.

The Lost Pieces of Me

In the corner
of my mind
Collecting dust
Is a version of me
I no longer get to be
Now that you're not
Here to see.

A cherished role
A part of my identity.
A core component
Of who I always fought to be.

It was once so vital
and now so veiled
from view in
this new reality.

And I'm still figuring out
How to mourn the pieces of me
That no longer fit together
In the way that I'd dreamed.

When nothing
Fits or feels
How I thought it would be,
I'm still figuring out
How to mourn the lost pieces of me.

Until You Experience It Yourself

You don't know until you experience it
For yourself.
Until you are surveying the
Shattered surface of your heart,
Salvaging what you can with no idea
Where to start.

You don't know until you experience it
For yourself.
Until you learn how a heart
Can feel both
Impossibly heavy and impossibly empty
All at once.

You don't know until you experience it
For yourself,
Until you feel how pain takes up residence
And space,
How it demands attention and energy
How it takes and takes,
Often at an exhausting pace.

It's the truth that every hurting heart
knows too well:

"You don't know
Until you experience it
For yourself."

Forward and Back

Grief is personal,
different for each of us
but so similar is the sense
of loneliness
that settles in
to each broken heart
searching for a way
through the hurt
forward,
forward
but reluctantly looking
back
back
before the pain.
before they left.
back.
begging to go
back
more time
back
one more "I love you"
just one more moment
then, we could move forward
but we can't go
back
time ticks on
life goes on
people move on
but we hold so tightly
to the past
fighting to move forward
but begging to go
back.

Rest

Sometimes, I want to
put these thoughts
In a box marked
"To be sorted through later".

Some days, I don't have
The capacity to look through
This pain written onto
The pages of my heart like paper.

Some things, I know
I can return to
On a day when it feels
A little easier to face.

And I think that's okay
To take some time,
To take a moment
To find my pace.

To look through it all,
To sort through it all,
But maybe just not today.

Hurting, but Here

And the heart
bravely replied,
"I'm hurting,
But I'm here."

Section Two:

The Ebbs and Flows

To Mourn the Memories

I've begun to make room
to mourn the memories
I thought I'd get to make with you.

My tears observing
The "what could have been"s
And this now-familiar wound.

I cycle through them.
I imagine them.
I ache over them.
I grieve them.

They were supposed to be here too,
These moments were supposed to
Happen with you.

So, whenever my heart needs
To feel the pain
Of that hard-to-face truth,

I've learned to take time to process,
To make room,
To mourn the memories
I thought I'd get to make with you.

Stars and Skies

I stepped outside
Into the cool night air,
To catch my breath
And catch a glimpse of
The stars shining there.

They've held vigil for me,
Their light gentle and steady
The night quiet and watchful,
Not expecting anything from me.

I can rest here a moment
And wrestle with the pain
Lament over how quickly
Everything can change.

And beneath this immense sky
I can ask God "Why?"
Why do we have to face
Such heartbreaking goodbyes?

And surrounded by
A blanket of midnight black,
I ask for the strength
I so desperately lack.

In the night,
I see stars glimmer
Bearing witness to the dark,
I see them continue to shine
And fill the skies
With their hopeful spark.

They show me that light
Still remains in these sorrowful spaces
And that's helped sustain my soul
For the hardships it faces.

Wave after Wave

The ache was so subtle,
an occasional hurt.
gradual until it wasn't.
tolerable until it wasn't.
hidden until it wasn't.

Grief slowly building up
until nothing could stop it
from tumbling
tumbling
down.

Ebbing and flowing
wave after wave…
grief overflowing
in a sea of heartbreak.

A Note to My Past Self

If I could go back
And tell you
About this pain,

About the hole in
your heart it would
create,
It still wouldn't
prepare you
For this journey you
would take.

So please proceed
gently
With your grief-
stricken heart.
There's no set way to
do this and no
prescribed way to
start.

It'll change and
evolve, and it's more
than okay
To adjust to grief's
presence in
Your own way.

So, please
allow yourself time
And allow yourself
space
To grieve and to
process
At your own pace.

Vulnerable

Being vulnerable is hard
Because once you share
That piece of your
hurting heart,
You have no control
Over how it's received
Or how they interpret
What they think they
see.

It takes a lot of courage
To extend your heart,
Like an outstretched
hand
In hopes that it might
help others understand
As though every beat is
saying
"This is how it's been
for me.
Please see me.
Please see me..."

<u>Happy</u>

And when rays of joy
Make my heart feel warm and free,
It's not long before
Thick clouds of anxiety
Cause doubt
To wash all over me,
Casting darkness over
Everything that I see.

But just a moment ago,
It was so sunny.
Just a moment ago,
I felt hopeful for what could be.

Why am I so afraid to feel happy?
Afraid it will be taken
Away from me?
Why am I so afraid to feel happy?

Is everyone afraid to feel happy?

Rain and Ruin

The rain tries its
best to relax
My storming
mind.
I feel it wash over
me,
Soaking into the
pain I planted,
The soil I
sorrowed over.

Now, all I see
Is rain and ruin,
But maybe one
day
It'll feel more like
Renewal and
reunion.

Grief Time

Some days, it feels like
It just happened yesterday.
Others, it feels
Impossibly distant
and far away.

But one thing
I know to be true:
Time moves
so differently
without you.

The Memories

The memories may soften
A little with time,
But the moments are engrained
On our hearts and our minds.
You may struggle
to remember specifics,
But you'll always
remember the love.

You won't forget.
You won't.

The love is there.
It is.

When I Parent but You're Not There to See It

I have kids of my own now,
They're growing so fast
I cling to the moments
Afraid they won't last
My encounter with loss
Is a shadow that's cast:
When I parent but you're
Not there to see it.

When I soothe with sweet songs
That you used to play.
When I teach them the wisdom
Of things you would say
When I tell them
My love for them
Grows more each day:
When I parent but you're
Not there to see it.

When I offer advice or
A listening ear
When they fill me
With such pride that I shed a tear
When I see every doubt
And calm every fear:
When I parent but you're
Not there to see it.

When I see all the holidays
Through their awe-filled eyes.
When they say something
So profound I'm taken by surprise
When I get to be part of
Their lows and their highs:
When I parent but you're
Not there to see it.

There'll be so many moments
You should have been there for
Moments my heart
Still laments and still yearns for
Oh, but I know your love lives
Deep in my core:
When I parent but you're
Not there to see it.

Sometimes what we plant,
We are not there to see,
At least not in the way
We envisioned we'd be.
So, I'll invest in my kids
Like you invested in me.

The love will be rooted.
The love will be deep.
The love will be our blooming legacies.
The love will bear witness
To this family tree.
When I parent,
I'll hope that they see it.

When I parent,
I'll hope somehow, you see it.

Love and Loss

Love changes you.
Loss changes you.
As we live, we find a way
To balance the two.

<u>Vital</u>

We've made a home in a
broken world full of
broken-hearted people.
May that be enough
To remind us how vital it is
To love one another.

Another's Pain

Another's pain
May be loud
But so often it's quiet
And if we don't
Stop and listen,
We might miss it.
May we practice
The pause.
May we always
Make the effort
To listen for it.

Loss Changes You

Loss changes you and it changes how
You see the world around you
It shifts your point of view.
It impacts everything you do.

You become more
Tender-hearted and aware
Of the hearts around you
Who feel shattered beyond repair.

You become more
Open-minded and alert
To the pain of those
Who have known worlds of hurt.

Because loss changes you
And it changes how
You see the people around you.
It helps you break through
Walls to tend to the wounds
And witness the hardships
Others have gone through.

Where Would We Be Without the Caregivers?

Their hearts so full
Of warmth and care
They step in and provide
Like an answered prayer.
Their eyes so full
Of empathy,
They hold hands
And hold space
For the hurting to feel seen.
Their souls so full
Of sincerity,
The first to give
And the first to pour out,
Anticipating every need.
Who step in
To comfort, to cover,
To soothe and to nurture,
To bear witness
To the pain of another.
Who lose sleep
Ever serving, pouring
From an empty cup
As they hold nocturnal vigil
When no one else is up.
Who are there
For every painful breath
And every tear cried.
Their grace, a loving guide
The bedrock at the bedside.

Oh, where would we be
Without the caregivers?

The Power of Words

The power of words
Is magnified
When a heart is wounded
And alone in the darkness.

Either we can offer our words
As a source of warmth
A light, an exhale,
A hand of empathy.

Or our words can
Cut deeply and quickly
Recklessly and relentlessly

The words matter:
For your heart
And the one who hears them.
May we choose them carefully
and compassionately.
May we offer them freely
And lovingly.
May we receive them
Graciously.

Lights

And then I realized,
Just how many lights that we could be
Once adrift in the night,
now casting the light
To other hurt souls lost at sea.

To Be Reminded

I want to say their name,
I want to soak in memories,
I want to remember.
I want to be reminded.

So, when you are around me,
Please don't be scared
To say their name
To share a memory,
To remember,
To be reminded.

Looking In

The car used to be
My place to cry
Watching the road
Slip past me
As the tears slipped
From my eyes

But yesterday,
The car was
A comfort,
A place to talk to you,
To tell you about my day
To tell you how much I miss you.

To open that piece of myself
That had been closed up
And darkened.
To let in a little light
And a little conversation
With my favorite person.

So, I'll let the light in
and imagine
you're listening.

I'll feel the
Light and
your love
both looking in.

<u>Comfort</u>

Words that bring
Hope and comfort
To my aching heart:

"You are so much like him."

__Support__

May we make
the most of
our moments:
To love.
To encourage.
To comfort
To support.

And when we need it most,
may we do our best to accept:
Love.
Encouragement.
Comfort.
Support.

I See You

when you listen as someone
pours out all
they've tried to hide away.
When you sit with someone
Through hardship
Without trying
To dictate their pace.
You get the chance
For your actions to say,
"I see you."
"I see you."
"I see you."

Section Three:

The Gentle Rain

I Allow Myself

I allow myself
to feel the underlying sorrow
in the moments I celebrate,
to acknowledge the ache
and the tension
that love and loss make.

I allow myself
To mourn the memories
We won't get to share
and to process the pain
of you not being there.

I allow myself
to lament the changes
in my identity,
to miss the pieces of myself
that you alone brought out of me.

And...

I allow myself
To soak in a cherished memory
and find long-awaited comfort there
when my heart is ready.

I allow myself
To look for your love
And seek your presence each day.
To learn how love
continues in unexpectedly magical ways.

I allow myself
to feel awed by the world,
by music and art and the trees,
and to feel surprised
by joy's ability
to still come and find me.

And perhaps most importantly,
With every fiber of my being:
I allow my heart
to be a home for love
despite its unexpected visitor,
grief.

Heart Lessons

I've found that as my heart
Has been broken open,
It has made me more aware
Of the fleeting and fragile beauty
Of the world around me.
It has filled me with a profound urgency
To appreciate the love I've been given.

It has challenged me
To honor the love
Of those I've lost
While acknowledging the way
Their love can still be found each day.

The Possibility

I always find myself hoping
That the right sound or smell
Could unlock a moment,
Could free a memory from
Deep inside of me
And feel like a piece of you
Returned to me.
I'll keep my heart open to the possibility…

That Song Came on Today

That song came on today.
The one you loved.
The one we listened to together,
The one whose melody mingles
with so many of our memories.
A soundtrack in the background of our days.

That song came on today.
The one that stops me in my tracks.
The one I have to skip sometimes
The one that sings about you
in so many ways.

That song came on today.
The one that hurts my heart to hear.
The one that lives deep in my core.
The one that transports me back
To days of singing it with you.

But that song came on today,
The one you loved.
And I sang along.
Some days,
I can still sing along.
I hope you're singing too.

Senses

Today, I thought of
you, And I felt
comforted By your
presence.

I could almost see
The light of your smile
Soothing my soul.

I could almost hear
The sound of your voice
Steady and full.

I could almost feel
Your hand reaching for mine
And holding tightly.

I could almost smell
The scent of pines,
Where we sat surrounded
by the trees.

I could almost taste
The coffee as we
Talked so freely.

I could sense
Your love so fully
Through this moment
So vividly.

And I know you're with me.
I know somehow, you're with me.
And I'll find you in my heart,
In our memories.

Please Never Forget

Please never forget
How brave it is
To continue to show up
In a story
that looks so
Different than what
You thought it'd be.

Please never forget
How brave it is
To dream up next chapters
While honoring the ones
That closed so painfully.

Please never forget
How brave it is,
To continue
To explore next pages
Despite feeling
Fear and anxiety.

Please never forget
How brave it is,
To hope and dream
Amidst the uncertainty.

Grief Has Taught Me

Grief has taught me
To honor and acknowledge love
With supreme gratitude and urgency,
Whether that's through new moments
Or long-cherished memories.

Grief has taught me
That love is our
Most valuable currency,
May we invest in our chances
To share it, often and willingly.
Overflow it into the hearts
Of the people we love steadily.

Grief has taught me
That this life is marked
By love, by its ability
To make a home within
Even the most broken
Of hearts as it shines
Into the darkest
Seasons so vividly.

Grief has taught me
That when I'm ready
I have the opportunity
To carry loves and legacies
Within me.
To honor the tension
Of love and loss courageously.
A keeper of stories.
A guardian of memories.
A witness of love persisting,
Beautifully and boldly.

To Make a Heart a Home

This heart
Houses the moments
That make my life whole.
This heart
Guards the memories
That feel like home.

Hope's Forms

Today, hope looked like
A ray of sunlight
Meeting my tired eyes,
As they scanned the skies.

Yesterday, hope sounded like
Laughter and song
And the joy that I felt
To be singing along.

The day before, hope felt like
A hand gently squeezing mine
An act of comfort that soothed
My soul in ways I can't fully define.

Hope rises in many forms.
It evolves in what
It looks like
It sounds like
It feels like

It gives me the strength to say,
"How will hope find me today?"
It gives me the courage to say,
"How will I find hope today?"

A Hard-Fought Spring

I look out my window,
To see what today may bring
I am greeted by rays
Of a hard-fought spring.
I hear the birds,
And they still have songs to sing
And maybe I do too,
Despite everything.

The Start

May this be
The start of a story
That will continue through you,
A love that overflows
Into all that you do.

Because this love
Is forever
And this love
Is for you.

This love is your legacy
of stories old and new
A testament to
everything you've
grown through.

It Matters

May tender hearts
Hold tightly to this
Important truth:

They were here,
And it mattered.

You are here,
And it matters.

Every heart that's
been touched
And every trial
gone through.

Their presence
has mattered
And yours does too,

May this bring new hope
into all that you do.

I Carry

I carry the grief with me,
It won't always look
How I think it should be
But it's constant and steady,
And when it knocks,
I'll try to be ready.

It won't always come
Through tears.
It won't always look
The same through the years
But in one way or another,
I carry grief with me.

I carry the love with me,
It won't always look
How I think it should be
But it's constant and steady
And when it knocks,
I'll try to be ready.

It's a song my heart sings
And the world hears
It's a story my soul carries
Despite all its fears.

But in one way or another,
I carry love with me.

Oh, to carry them both
Is my heart's hardest journey.
But I don't walk alone.
I know you'll be with me.

So, until we meet again,
I'll carry the grief.
I'll carry the love.
I'll carry them with me.
Oh, I'll carry you with me

Space

I will give grief
The space it needs
To express the love,
To endure the loss,
And to envision a future that,
Despite all odds,
Still looks
Hopeful,
Faithful,
And beautiful.

What If

What if we started
Treating time
As the fleeting friend that it is?
Would it help us slow down,
To stop and reflect,
To really cherish it?

Would it help us
Be present
And more aware of it?

How would that change
our moments?
How we love and how we live?

What if we started treating time
As the fleeting friend that it is?

Summer Rain

The sun's rays greet me
On these long summer days
Warm and inviting,
I do my best to fix my
gaze, But the sadness feels
like A subtle summer rain
Soaking through to the bone
Flooding into my heart
In ways I can't explain.

But maybe part of living
Is learning to embrace
The unexpected weather
And how it brings about such change.
Both for the soil
And the surface
And the love that still remains.
May it saturate every inch of this heart
And all that it contains.

Version of Me

This is a version of myself
I never envisioned I'd be:

The version that walked
Through some of the darkest days
And most painful realities.

The version that lost
so many plans for the future
And mourned countless broken dreams.

The version that felt
Overwhelmed and unsure,
and unraveled at the seams.

The version that aged
A   thousand   lifetimes
Who wrestled with loss
And was weathered by grief.

The version that faced
The shifting waves,
the ebbs and flows
that no one else could see.

The version that changed
And will change again
Who's felt love, loss,
And everything between.

But, despite the changes,
There's so much more
to this unexpected version of me:

I see hope.
I see love.
I see parts of the old me.
I see the pieces coming together
Despite the uncertainty.

I see how much my heart
Continues to learn
And grow and beat
With such tender resiliency.
And I can say with renewed perspective
with appreciation and clarity:

This is a version of myself
I never envisioned I'd be.

Support System

You were starlight
In my sorrow,
And I will never be able
To thank you

For the hope you helped
Dawn in my heart
Just by being present
And helping me through.

A Truth to Soothe You

I needed to be reminded
That the rain doesn't only downpour,
It can be gentle too.
May that be a truth
That soothes you too.

Part of Me

There's so much to sort through
And process along the way,
Now I understand why
The grief must stay.

And over time
as I've gotten
To know my grief,
I'm not as afraid of it
as I used to be.

It's a part of me.
It's a part of me

Beautiful Heart

Beautiful heart,
Despite all you've been through,
So much love
Still grows in you.

Section Four:

The Hope That Grows

A Cloudy Day in the Month of June

It was an overcast day
In the month of June,
With Father's Day approaching
Much too soon.

The days have been sunny
Full of warmth
and full of light,
There hasn't been a whisper
Of rain in sight.

But it's like the sky took
notice
Of the rain within me
And brought a cloudy covering
Of tender empathy.

And as the rain began to fall
So slowly and still
I gave my tears permission
To fall at will.

And there we were,
My aching heart
And an aching sky

Experiencing the
gentle comfort
of allowing ourselves
To cry.

Here and There

I sit in silence and prepare my heart
To watch the time on the clock
When my world tore apart.
I take note of it every year, on this day
Of the moment you left us
And how there was still so much to say.

I look up to the sky, my heart aches like a tender bruise
Your absence every bit as loud as the day we lost you.
But as I look up and search for words to pray
Deep in my bones, I know this is true:

The Lord is here with me
And He's also there with you.
He's helping and guiding me
And He's also taking care of you.

Oh, what a beautiful thought to hold on to.

His love resides with both of us
His love connects us too.
Because the Lord is here with me
And He's also there with you.

The Palpable Reminder

There was a time when
I tried to rush my grief
As though its presence
Should only be temporary.

But now I'm learning
That grief is a part of me,
And it's okay to talk about
And share that vulnerability.

Now I'm seeing
The pain's not only
True of my story,
Bearing witness to the losses
That other hearts carry.

For grief's a palpable reminder
To you and to me
That the love is forever,
And the love is deep.
The stories we carry
And memories we keep,

They matter immensely.

Subtle Healing

Soft sunlight meeting tired eyes.
Long awaited exhales
And joy that takes you by surprise.

Color returning
To the world that you see.
Potential returning
To what you think life could be.

Hope for tomorrow
Despite darkness that fell
And the strength to face
A blank page
With another story to tell.

Subtle healing peeking over the horizon
Of your weary heart.

It may feel overwhelming,
But it's a beautiful place to start.

As You Grieve

May this comfort you
As you grieve
To know that the love
Will never leave.

Chapters to be Cherished

Because when you were here,
You loved with such
Intentionality and consistency,
An integral part of our family tapestry.

And stories of love and legacies
Are meant

To be shared.
To be told.
To be cherished.
To be carried.

The Story Continues

Lives divided into chapters
And sung like soundtracks.
We share our stories
And find our harmonies,
Though our hands may
Shake as we write them,
and our voices may quake
As we sing them.

But this is how the story continues.
This is how we share
The memories we've guarded
And the moments we've tended
And the ways our hearts
Have been wounded and mended.
This is how the story continues.
Through me and through you.
This is how their story continues.
This is how our story continues.

<u>Time</u>

So scared of time.
So aware of time.
So desperate for time.
So grateful for time.

To Hope

To hope is so brave.
To hope is to show up
despite the pain.
To hope is to remember
in the darkness,
The good
of the light remains
Even when,
especially when
It feels like things
will never be the same.

In A Memory

Today,
I visited you in a memory.
something I couldn't yet do
in the early days of grief,
I let my heart wander
let my mind roam free
in the way that it used to be,
to feel your presence,
so persistent, so steady
to reflect, to remember
and see you're still with me.
I knew that those moments
would be waiting when I was ready.
So today,
I visited you in a memory.

Soundtracks

Our lives are made up
Of songs that we've sung,
The soundtracks of our days.

The ones that remember
the things that have stung,
The ones that still hurt
when we press play.

Nostalgia drifts through
As I think of you
And a deep and palpable ache.
But each melody's tied
With a memory
That time and loss
Simply cannot break.

I let them harmonize
as tears dance in my eyes,
their presence so vivid and strong.

These songs and these lyrics,
a home for my heart
and a place where
yours too will belong.

Like a hymn of hope,
I tune in to the love,
I feel the words deep in my bones.

These songs mark the time
and the moments and
each one reminds me
that I'm not alone.

The Lyrics

Maybe our lives
Get to play a small part
In the lyrics that sing
To another person's heart.

The pain we go through
The melody our stories create,
We may never know how much
Of a difference it makes.

Stained Glass Legacies

A rock through a window,
Thrown mercilessly fast and unexpectedly
Recklessly, senselessly
Loss shatters our reality
Disturbs any sense of normalcy
we look over the wreckage
We are forced to reflect
On what we see

Can we salvage the memory? The legacy?
Collecting recollections,
Finite fragments
Or figments of my imagination?
Now I'm the keeper of these stories.

Life is so fleeting and fragile.
We are all so fleeting and fragile.
I sit in the debris, the heaviness of grief
Terrified of losing
Even one piece

Disarray and despair
Hearts beyond any hope of repair.
To restore that which can't be restored,
The broken realities of a broken world.

How do I do this without you?
How does anyone continue
In a story that ended before it was supposed to?

And yet...
We show up in the shattered places,
In the darkest of spaces
To sort through what remains.

Putting it back together
Will be a lifelong effort,
An ancestral alignment.

A mosaic of stained-glass souls,
Crafted in everyday chaos
Lined with loss, every person a piece
Purposefully placed
With pride in the family landscape

You were here and it mattered.
And what I see,
Is what my children will see,
And their children will see.

And it'll grow with
The years and tears of ancestry

Love and legacy
Born out of a broken story,
Persisting and persevering
Through our family's history
Shining in its shattered vibrancy.

It's you. It's me.
It's love. It's family.
It's life in its tragic urgency.
And, oh, it's beautiful.
I wish you could see.

<u>The Words</u>

And even though
I may not hear
The words
"I'm proud of you."
I'll do my best
To make it true
With everything I do.

Forever Grief

I know it may
Feel daunting
To think of grief as "forever",
But it allows your heart
To acknowledge that
Love cannot be severed.

It remains and our grief
Bears witness
To this truth,
We learn to honor its presence
As we grow and change too.

It shows our hearts
It's okay to feel
The weight of this pain,
To process and continue
In our own way
And pace.

"No timeline"
Gives our aching hearts
Much-needed space
To learn how to carry it
And navigate this space.

Still Here

There will be days
When hope's rays
Warmly envelop your soul
A solace of sunrise
Making it easy to feel whole.

There will be days
When hope's light
Is hidden, out of sight
Tucked away behind
A cold dark blanket of moonlight.

But most days
Hope will rise on a heart slowly
Soft and patient
Appearing so subtly
A dance on the breeze,
Bears witness to the
hues and hymns
of the changing leaves,
Planted firmly amongst the trees
To meet weary travelers
And offer reprieve
From the things the darkness has tried
To make them believe.

It speaks to our fear,
Hope gently glimmers
Like a slow burn it simmers,
Flickering faithfully, it whispers:
"I'm still here. Still here."

I've Been Waiting

And in the stillness
of morning
My heart aches with the possibility
Of renewed strength for another day
Of the hope splintering through
My heart like an open windowpane
For another chance
to begin again.
To try again.
To rise again.

Oh, hope:

I've been waiting.
Please dawn gently.

Joy after Loss

Joy after loss
Is not a betrayal.
The pain you've felt
Does not have to shut
the door
Of your shattered heart
To the possibility of
Something beautiful
Awakening within
Your weary soul.

This joy is yours,
It is deepened
By everything you've
been through.
This joy is yours,
It'll honor every
moment,
The old and the new.
This joy is yours.
To sustain and
strengthen all you do.
It's yours.
Don't let the darkness
Take it from you.

Hope, Too

And in the same place
That grief greeted me

Hope has begun to knock, too.
They both live within
This heavy heart
As I process
Life without you.

Hope has begun to knock, too.
Oh, how I desperately needed it to.

And in the same place
That grief greeted me
Hope has begun to knock, too.

My Heart Will Always Look for You

My heart in all its brokenness
Will always look for you.
Chasing down a familiar scent
Following the trail of a favorite memory,
Relentless in its pursuit.

Every morning, feeling the ache
Of that now familiar wound.
Of navigating a life, a story
Whose chapters were too few.

But what a legacy you've left
In the chapters you were here,
And what a story that you've left
A love that perseveres.

My heart in all its hopefulness
Will always look for you.
Cherishing those sometimes-painful memories,
Holding them tightly
To feel you with me too.

Your absence brings
A deep and lingering ache,
But your love persists here too,
A bond that will never break
That will comfort and continue.

So, it seems no matter what I do,
My heart will always look for you,
In everything I do,
In every memory old and new.

My heart will always look for you.

Worth Fighting For

And may you
Allow fresh rays of hope
To dawn before
your tired eyes,
To remind you that
Light can still find you
And take you by surprise.
Let it rise in your heart
Let it rise in your core
To remind you there's
Still so much
Worth fighting for.

Your heart is worth fighting for.
Your healing is worth fighting for.

Dawn breaks on our heartbreak,
And, oh, it's worth fighting for.

Poetry/Journaling Prompts for the Aching Heart

I am such a firm believer in the power of words and poetry. It is a space where we can explore our experiences and reflect on our emotions. And it's often a place where we can find comfort, connection, and community.

Writing has been a huge part of my personal processing. It has always felt like a safe space for me to start to make sense of my circumstances. That blank page has been a friend to me more times than I can count.

That is the reason that it has been important to me to include writing and journaling prompts for all of you as well.

What I love about poetry and journaling is that they are accessible to everyone. Whether you are an aspiring writer or can't remember the last time you put pen to paper, this section is for you.

The prompts are meant to be a starting point.

My hope is that they can feel like a gentle friend sitting across from you, encouraging you to reflect and write from the heart about what you've been going through.

That's another beautiful thing about writing: you can share your words with a friend if you'd like (or a therapist, support group, or family member). Or the words you write can be just for you. It is entirely up to you.

Heartbreak and hardship often bring us face to face with new and challenging realities.

And as we grieve and process and ache, may we find that despite all odds:

The love we have received from those we've lost is ours to keep forever: it continues.

The story of their life that they shared with us is a legacy that they have nurtured and grown in each of our hearts: it continues.

The love continues through me. The love continues through you.

May we take our time as we honor and process each chapter. May we take our time as we nurture a deep hope for the chapters that we have yet to write.

Hurting and healing alongside you,

Liz

Poetry/Journaling Prompts for the Aching Heart

Prompt One: Music and Memories

Music and memories have a way of weaving themselves together in our hearts. A song can transport us back to a specific moment with a sharp and sometimes painful clarity.

Reflect on the songs that take you back to a moment in your life's soundtrack. Explore the thoughts and feelings the melody resurfaces for you. Write in as much detail as you can about why the song has mattered so much to you. Maybe the song you choose fills you with nostalgia or takes you back to a previous version of yourself. Maybe the song is one that marked a big milestone or one that helped you through a hard time. (Some songs may be too painful to revisit in this way, and that's okay. It's okay if, for some songs, it feels too difficult to press play right now.)

Alternatively, you can explore why music in general has been a safe space to you or how it has added vibrancy to your moments.

Poetry/Journaling Prompts for the Aching Heart

Prompt Two: Grief and love continue

This book is based on the idea that while grief may continue, the love we were given does too.

How have you continued to experience grief in your day to day? How has it changed? How has it stayed the same?

How has your perspective of grief changed as you navigate your own experience with loss?

Now, flip the question: How have you continued to experience their love day to day? How has it changed? How has it stayed the same?

How has your perspective of love changed as you navigate your own experience with loss?

Allow your thoughts to join together and form one poem in whatever order you choose.

Poetry/Journaling Prompts for the Aching Heart

Prompt Three: A Keeper of the Sentimental

Whether we collect physical items or not, most of us are collectors of the sentimental moments we've had over the years.

Imagine you are sorting through a "memory box" of your sentimental moments. How do you feel as you look through? Which ones stand out the most? Which ones have been pushed to the bottom? Which ones do you ache to remember? Which ones remain on the top to revisit again and again?

Take your time as you do this mental sorting, and when you're ready, journal or write a poem about what you've found.

Poetry/Journaling Prompts for the Aching Heart

Prompt Four: Seen in our Sorrow

As human beings, we all ache to feel seen and understood, especially in our deepest and darkest moments.

Write a poem about the things that have made you feel the most "seen" in your sorrow. This can also be a poem of appreciation for a friend or supportive person who has made a difference in your life. (If you feel up to it, you could even share it with them. It's totally up to you.)

Poetry/Journaling Prompts for the Aching Heart

Prompt Five: The Layers of Loss We Grieve Along the Way

Grief shows us that there are so many additional layers to loss that we mourn along the way: we mourn the memories we don't get to make, the future we thought we would get to have, the moments we no longer get to share, and so much more.

Allowing ourselves to mourn these additional losses can be such a helpful part of our processing.

What are some of the layers of loss that your grief journey has revealed to you along the way?

How have these presented themselves in your day to day?

Poetry/Journaling Prompts for the Aching Heart

Prompt Six: Visiting in a Memory

Some days, I can almost transport myself back to a memory. I allow the nostalgia to guide me. I allow my heart to ache and to feel how much this moment has always meant to me. And I linger there.

This was not something I could do in the early stages of grief, but it is something I was able to come back to when my heart was ready.

If your heart feels ready, allow yourself to go and "visit" a memory. Describe what you see, who you're with, what's happening, and why this moment has mattered so much to you. (This can be the entire poetry/ journaling prompt, or it can be the first paragraph or stanza as you stroll through and connect a few additional memories.)

Allow the words to flow in a way that feels helpful to you.

Poetry/Journaling Prompts for the Aching Heart

Prompt Seven: Grief Changes

Grief trickles its way into our days in a million little ways. But every time that it does, it has soaked down to my soul and changed me.

Grief has changed the way I react to the pain of the broken hearts around me. It has ushered in a deeper empathy. It has also changed the way I care for others: it has added an urgency to the way I love and care for the people around me.

On the flip side, grief has also changed the way I react to uncertainty, and it can be easy for me to slip into anxiety. But being aware of this change helps me understand myself a bit better and work to put my faith in front of my fear.

As you prepare to write, reflect on what changes grief has brought about in you.

Poetry/Journaling Prompts for the Aching Heart

Prompt Eight: Bringing the pieces together again

When our hearts are shattered open, we are left to look at the pieces scattered around us. We are left to lament the loss as we try and figure out how we could ever possibly make sense of it all and put it back together again.

As you have started to pick up the pieces of your heart, what have you learned about how they can come together again? What is the uniting force? What is the hope that helps guide your hand as you sort through each piece and decide what comes next?

Poetry/Journaling Prompts for the Aching Heart

Prompt Nine: Another Unexpected Guest: Joy

In "I Look to the Mourning Sky", I wrote about how grief enters our lives and lingers like an unexpected guest. It took a lot of time for me to let the grief in and start honoring my processing.

Now, I find that I often feel conflicted by the arrival of another unexpected guest: joy. Maybe, you've felt that tension, too. Or maybe you are still waiting for the day when you do.

As you prepare to write, imagine what it would feel like to be greeted by this unexpected guest. What would you say? Would you let joy in? How would it coexist in the same space as your pain?

Poetry/Journaling Prompts for the Aching Heart

Prompt Ten: A Letter to My Grieving Self

There is such power in letter writing. This prompt offers two different perspectives and approaches. Choose whichever feels right to you.

Option 1: If you are freshly grieving (and feel up to an exercise like this), write to your future self. Feel free to ask your questions and express your doubts. Describe what this has felt like and how it's changed you. Reflect on the painful and challenging things that you find yourself going through. (This could even be a letter that you tuck away and respond to later as described in the next option.)

Option 2: If you are further along in your grieving, write to your past self who is in fresh loss. How would you validate what and how they're feeling? How would you gently encourage them as they're processing? Where would you tell them you've been finding hope?

Poetry/Journaling Prompts for the Aching Heart

Prompt Eleven: Stories Continued

Each of us has a unique story. And beautifully, they are all part of a much bigger story of love and connection.

Who are some people who have greatly impacted your life's story? How has their role in your story continued to shape and nurture you, even if they are no longer here?

What are some ways that you hope to add to and impact the stories of the people around you? Which chapters of your story do you hope to pass on to others, to be continued?

Poetry/Journaling Prompts for the Aching Heart

Prompt Twelve: The Gentle Rain

When I first began writing this book,
I loved to imagine a gentle, soothing
summer rain. I pictured the sun
peeking out from the clouds as the
rain fell softly to the ground.

I thought about how our hearts are
often home to so many complicated
realities: love and loss, grief and
gratitude, pain and purpose, joy and
sorrow.

To me, a gentle rain is a therapeutic
experience. It is something that
honors the tension we feel as human
beings as we acknowledge and honor
the heartwarming and the
heartbreaking moments we've been
given.

As you prepare to write, reflect on
this: what has felt like a gentle
rain to your aching heart in this
season? What has brought unexpected
healing? What has watered the hope
you've planted? What has soaked
through and saturated that darkness
in a way that reminded you of the
Light?

Thank you for being here with me and for reading.

I hope that this book is a reminder to you that your pain and your processing matter.

And while I know our grief stories are different, I hope that you found something here that resonated with your aching heart and made you feel a little less alone as you navigate the chapters of yours.

Hurting and healing alongside you,

Liz

About The Author

Liz Newman is a blogger and a poet from the Midwest who writes primarily on grief, faith, life, and relationships. Her book "I Look to the Mourning Sky" received a Readers ' Favorite Bronze Medal in 2022 in the Inspirational Poetry category. Her words have been shared on "Her View from Home", "Read Poetry", "Love What Matters", and "The Mighty." They have also appeared in The London Underground. She believes in the power of words to comfort, connect, and bring hope. Her journey through grief has been a humbling reminder of how desperately we all need grace and each other. She writes with the hope that her words can meet people right where they are and make them feel seen in their own difficult seasons.

Printed in Great Britain
by Amazon